EMBRACE GRATITUDE

100 Lessons to Enhance your Life by Practicing Gratitude Every Day

David George Brooke

Published by Pacelli Publishing
Bellevue, Washington

Six-Word Lessons to Embrace Gratitude

Published by Pacelli Publishing
9905 Lake Washington Blvd. NE, #D-103
Bellevue, Washington 98004
PacelliPublishing.com

Cover and interior designed by Pacelli Publishing
Cover image by Zac Durant via Unsplash

ISBN-10: 1-933750-97-9
ISBN-13: 978-1-933750-97-2

Dedication

I dedicate this book to my mother Helene Brooke Rigger. While I only had the benefit of her parenting and guidance for a very short 30 years, she taught me to never give up on my dreams. Even though the line is used often, I never tired of her telling me, "David, you can do anything you want on this earth, if you just set your mind to it." Her influence on me has lasted my entire lifetime and has always been my source of inspiration and motivation. I know she is still watching me from above.

Contents

Introduction

When I was nineteen years old, I decided I wanted to be a speaker when I grew up. While it only took another forty-three years to get up the courage to fulfill that dream, I have never looked back, considering the impact that my speaking on gratitude has had.

Having given over 500 speeches in the last six years, people consistently ask me, "Can I get what you talked about in a book?" This book gives you an overview of what I talk about in my presentations: *Happiness Starts with Gratitude* and *Gratitude Creates Peak Performance.*

These snackable chunks of wisdom will give you a window into the overall power of gratitude and what embracing an "attitude of gratitude" mindset can give you. Feel free to read the entire book at one time or read and digest one or two messages each day.

It seems like the world has gotten more negative than ever before. Being happy is a choice we make in life just like choosing regular or decaf coffee. Choose gratitude and you will follow the path that I found to be so much more rewarding. Gratitude turns what you have into enough.

This book refers to a daily gratitude journal. I have published *The Brooker's Daily Gratitude Journal* for this purpose, or you may use any notebook or journal of your choice.

For more information on this and other books, speaking engagements or coaching services, go to my website at *ThatGratitudeGuy.com*

Embrace Gratitude and Enhance Your Life

1

Nothing is more precious than you.

The person in the mirror is the one relationship you have complete control over. The better you like and respect that person, the better your life will operate. Having a great relationship with yourself gives you the best protection available to guard against the negatives of life. Be grateful for knowing yourself well and respecting all that you do.

2

Give thanks for your mind/body.

Take the time every day to think specifically about gratitude for your mind and body. Gratitude gives you a stronger immune system, more energy, and more focus. The connection between mind and body is so important. The mind directs the body, and the body takes you where you want to go.

3

Focus on your many daily blessings.

Focusing on your blessings will always put you in a better mood and create a very positive mindset. For example, if two patients enter a hospital with the same disease, often the one with the positive attitude lives, while the one with the negative attitude dies. Use your gratitude thoughts, lists, and feelings to reinforce your positive attitude daily.

4

Concentrate on your family and friends.

Many people have achieved great levels of success and unfortunately have few friends and family to celebrate with. Your family and friends are so often the people who stick with you through thick and thin, and in so many cases know you better than anyone else. Be sure to reinforce those relationships on a regular basis. Show them how grateful you are to have them in your life.

5

Meditation for the here and now.

One of the biggest advantages of a meditation practice is that it helps you to experience the here and now. Your conversations, communication, and interactions will be so much more fulfilling when they are in the here and now, both literally and figuratively. Being grateful helps to keep you focused on the most important time in your life . . . now.

6

Always say yes to present moments.

Whenever someone asks for your time, instead of putting them off, say yes to that present moment. The present moment is like a gift--a present of your time and attention. You may not get another opportunity down the road. Being present will make you feel that you really impacted someone else's life.

7

Develop a prefight checklist every evening.

Organizing your day the night before will make your day go smoother. Develop a preflight checklist at night before you go to bed to ensure that your day will get off to a great start. You will sleep better also.

8

Let gratitude do the heavy lifting.

Life can be such a struggle at times, and it is so helpful to adopt a gratitude mindset that keeps you focused on what you have versus what you don't. Navigating the ups and downs and successfully handling the big challenges is so much easier with an "attitude of gratitude." It's like getting a power assist.

9

Do you see me, hear me?

I think most people want to be noticed and heard. It is so gratifying when someone pays attention to you and to your point of view. When you align yourself with gratitude, you are able to increase your self-confidence and that makes you more visible. You will notice that people will truly hear you.

10

Do I matter all that much?

A central question that comes up as people get older is, “Do I matter?” Gratitude helps you focus on your blessings and your abundance and that will give you a better sense of self, which makes you matter that much more. Gaining that self-confidence will give your life more purpose.

Clear Out Your Brain, Make Room

11

Don't say I'm sorry, seek forgiveness.

I have a friend who said some hurtful things. When he called to apologize, instead of saying "I'm sorry," he said, "I would like to ask for your forgiveness." It was such a loving way to repair our friendship, that I came to appreciate the value of seeking forgiveness. The friendship has been even stronger since that situation.

12

See the windshield, not rearview mirror.

The windshield on your car is about one hundred times bigger than the rearview mirror. It shows what is in front of you. What a great way to look at your life. Look out in front to see what is on the horizon. You can occasionally look in the rearview mirror to learn from the past, and if you see blue lights flashing, you should probably pull over. What's really important is what is in front of you.

13

Gratitude protects you from life's valleys.

I remember sleeping on a friend's piece of foam after my life had taken a significant turn downhill. Life is a series of hills and valleys and we learn the most important lessons in the valleys. When you're on top everyone knows your phone number, but when you're on the bottom nobody seems to remember. Gratitude is the best armor to protect you from the impact of life's ups and downs.

14

Don't fret over yesterday's old garbage.

When you have experienced negative events in your life, process them through your mind and leave them in the past. Just like yesterday's garbage, those negative thoughts and events are no longer needed or necessary to you. Send them out with the trash.

15

Don't keep on burning your finger.

Life has a way of teaching us lessons every day. In every difficult event or happening, one of the great things that happens is that there is always a lesson to be learned. Be sure to look for the lesson and don't touch that hot stove again. Be grateful for what life has taught you.

16

Make your strengths much more productive.

This may be one of the best lessons you can learn in life. Why do you not focus on your strengths? You can't be good at everything. Gratitude will direct you to the things that you do well and that will ensure much better outcomes in many areas of life.

17

Make all your weaknesses completely irrelevant.

When the boss says he wants to talk to you, it usually makes you think it is something negative. Why does your brain go there? I don't know, but it is best to forget about your weaknesses. Put your energy into what you are good at, you'll be much happier.

18

Zero in on what you have.

A gratitude mindset means that you just focus on what you have. When you write down your blessings it is nice to prioritize them. Each person can write their own list, and I think a lot of people would typically include their health, family, friends, and so on. To remember this, think about where you would be without any of these things.

19

More listening equals more gratitude engagement

When practicing a gratitude mindset, you are constantly focused on all of the positives in your life. By being a good listener, asking great questions, and truly being engaged in the conversation, you will find out a lot of information that will make you even more grateful. You can't learn anything when you are talking.

20

Tell me more, and what else?

If you are unsure of when to talk or enter the conversation, remember two three-word phrases that will guarantee a great talk. “Tell me more,” and “And what else?” will ensure that your conversation continues on and your learning progresses without an interruption. The people you’re talking to will think that you are the nicest person.

Be Very Patient with the Process

21

No goal is out of reach.

Goal setting is like having a road map and it has proven to be very effective in helping you on your journey through life. Always aim high. It has been proven that one of the mistakes people make when setting goals is NOT setting them high enough. You can do anything, if you just set your mind to it. Gratitude assists you in reaching those goals.

22

Patience is a virtue, like gratitude.

As gratitude guides you to focus on all that you have, a great side benefit is that it helps keep you patient. As you consistently focus on those wonderful things in your life, you will have a tendency to be more confident in the road ahead and you won't be in such a hurry.

23

You're not old, you are older.

Your self-talk and language are so important. Your ears hear what you say and that impacts your thinking. Something as simple as saying, "I'm older" instead of, "I'm old" can make a huge difference. You are the only one who controls your thinking. Your language directs your mind. Gratitude makes you feel younger, too.

24

Colonel Sanders, J.C. Penney, Ray Kroc

Colonel Sanders, J.C. Penney, and Ray Kroc all started very successful ventures late in life. It doesn't matter where you are when you want to restart your life. Many extremely successful people have dramatically changed their personal or professional lives later in life. As long as you are passionate about your quest, your age will not be a factor. After all, you are only as old as you feel. Furthermore, gratitude will keep you feeling younger.

25

What learning to fly taught me.

When you learn how to fly, they tell you to listen to your instructor. There may be a time that it saves your life. It pays to be grateful to the people who come along in your life to instruct you in the matters of living. These people/mentors/instructors might even save you a lot of pain.

26

Always listen to your flight instructor.

My flight instructor said, "Always believe your instruments, even when your brain says they are wrong." That simple statement saved me over and over again. Gratitude will help you to believe in yourself and the lessons your mentors have taught you along the way.

27

Minor course corrections in your life

The course of your life will have many twists and turns. There may be several major swings in your life, but generally your best course of life is to make minor course corrections and to not overreact and over-correct. When your mind is programmed with gratitude, the occasional big event will end up being something that is easily corrected.

28

Cord of wood theory in action

How do you put a cord of wood away? One piece of wood at a time. What a great way to tackle any project! Don't focus on the enormity of the project, just break it down into bite-sized pieces. Before you know it, the project will be done. Being grateful for the small steps helps avoid being overwhelmed.

29

500 speeches, and finally getting it

Recently someone heard a speech that I had given on gratitude. They said, "You were really good." I thanked them and reminded them that I had given over 500 speeches in the last five years. Practice makes perfect and gratitude keeps you humble.

30

25 years to become overnight success

You always appreciate what you worked hard for, more than something that came easy. When people say someone was an overnight success, in almost every case that person had to work many years to achieve that success. Being grateful helps you to focus on all of the steps that it took to achieve that success.

Gratitude Strengthens Your Relationship with You

31

It's your journey and yours only.

Whenever you are tempted to be jealous of someone else's path in life, just remember that your journey is yours only. Each person was given a unique set of skills and talents. Use gratitude to focus solely on the ways that you can best use your blessings, and don't worry about anyone else's.

32

Your relationship with you says everything.

The better you get to know the person in the mirror, the more everything in your life will improve. Your attitude, your self-confidence and your self-esteem all improve with a better view of you. A gratitude mindset will drive your feelings to a much higher level.

33

Establishing your direction and true destiny

When you find your direction and get grateful for your life, it is easier to find your true destiny. Sometimes it's as easy as remembering what you wanted to do when you grew up. Leaving a legacy is one of the most thoughtful things you can do. Gratitude can assist in that quest by showing you your strengths, motivations, and desires.

34

The Andrew Jackson $20 bill exercise

If you look at a twenty-dollar bill you will see Andrew Jackson on the front. Whether that bill is damaged, crushed, or stepped on, it is still worth $20. Don't ever let anyone make you feel that you are less than your full value. A gratitude mindset will help you to believe in your worth as well.

35

The biggest regret of the dying

When senior citizens were asked about their biggest regrets, the number one answer was, "I wish I would have taken more chances." Why would someone think that? Well, it may be that they didn't focus enough on what they had in their life. When you get grateful and focus on your gifts, you will appreciate your life more, and that helps to give you the courage to try new and exciting things. Another example of gratitude's power.

36

You just changed my life today.

There may be nothing more powerful on this earth than the ability to change another person's life. I am fortunate enough to be told this on a regular basis and it never gets old. By impacting other people's lives, you give your life so much more meaning.

37

Great gratitude exercise with 3x5 card

Rate your current day with a number between 1 and 10. After that, write down the three things you are most grateful for in your life at this moment. Silently reread the three things and then see if your number changes. Whenever I do this exercise for groups, at least half of the people see their number increase. Again, the power of gratitude.

38

Try to impress yourself, not others.

If you pay attention to human nature when you are talking to people, you will notice that most people just want to talk about themselves. If you are grateful for everything you have, you won't feel the need to talk about yourself. Besides, it's more fun to learn about other people. You can't learn anything when you're talking about you.

39

Take time to find your passion.

How do you find out what you are passionate about? Ask yourself the following questions: What did I want to be when I grew up? What would I do if I only had five years to live? What would I do if I had unlimited time and money? Answering these questions will help you to find your passion.

40

Finding purpose takes thought and contemplation.

When you have a good sense of yourself, and you have established an "attitude of gratitude" you have completed the first step. Step two is finding your passion (See Lesson 39). Mix those two steps with a lot of thought and you will find your purpose. If you still can't find it, repeat steps one and two, and spend more time contemplating. You'll figure it out.

Start Writing in a Gratitude Journal

41

Bullet points or complete sentences work.

When I am writing in my gratitude journal, I always write in complete sentences. It is fine to make a list of bullet points too. It is also helpful to write important events at the top of the page for emphasis. As long as you are listing all the things you are grateful for, you will feel the effects in your mind.

42

The value of the daily number

The daily number is a rating of your day from 1 to 10. It is a mystery why people feel so great on one day and so crummy on another. The daily number gives you a reading of how you are feeling each day, like taking your mental temperature. Writing in a gratitude journal every day will improve your daily numbers and fend off the negative gamma rays of life.

43

Prioritize your observations of daily gratitude.

When focusing on the positives in your life, it is helpful to prioritize your gratitude list from highest to lowest in importance. Your brain will automatically put the most emphasis on the items at the top of the list.

44

Special occasions mean no diary necessary.

My *Brooker's Daily Gratitude Journal* has two lines for current events and special occasions. This is a great place to put the day's happenings and avoids the need for a daily diary. You can also highlight those daily events by writing at the top of the page or in the margins. It's so nice to reference those events when you look back at your gratitude journal later.

45

Consistent entries create momentum and energy.

There may be nothing more important regarding your daily gratitude journal than being consistent and making daily entries. Just like any other muscle in the body, your brain will benefit greatly from the consistency you show by making entries every single day. It is called a DAILY gratitude journal for a reason.

46

Your gratitude intentions design the future.

Your gratitude intentions, or your gratitude for tomorrow, is a way to program your brain to be grateful for something that hasn't even happened yet. Your subconscious mind cannot distinguish what you think has happened and what actually has happened. You can then direct your future from the present by writing your gratitude intentions today.

47

Remember to include all important elements.

While I want people to come up with their own gratitude aspects, I think it is important to remember some of the "basics" in your life. Most entries will probably include topics such as health, family, friends, jobs, careers, spirituality, and so on.

48

Add additional gratitude feelings during day.

When something happens during the day, it is a great idea to make some notes in the margin of your journal. You can add anything that is significant, special, or worth noting. Some people even write down a quick note to themselves to add to the gratitude journal later.

49

Journal to pause, learn, and reflect.

After you have written in your gratitude journal over a period of time, you can look back and see what happened on various days in your past. This can be very helpful with a current issue you may be dealing with. You can reference something that worked back then, and apply it to a current situation.

50

Write in morning, read at night.

I generally recommend that you write in your gratitude journal in the morning to start your day off with the positive feelings that gratitude will create. It is then handy to read your entries in the evening before you go to bed. The more you reinforce your expressions of gratitude, the more it will plant them permanently in your brain.

Daily Expressions of Appreciation and Gratitude

51

Make a list of blessings daily.

It is so easy to go down a negative path considering the fact that a lot of life can be very negative. By making a list of your blessings every day, you will blunt the forces that create negative feelings and attitudes. You can incorporate your list into your daily gratitude journal entries to further reinforce your feelings of seeing the upside of everything.

52

Share what's on your gratitude list.

When you share your goals and objectives with other people, you will have a much higher chance of accomplishing your objectives because it holds you accountable. By sharing your gratitude list, it further cements it in your mind by including other people in the thought process.

53

Show love and appreciation for parents.

Without your parents, you would not exist. Being grateful for your parents and expressing it frequently will go a long way to let them know how much you fully appreciate the role that they played in your life. Raising a child is one of the hardest jobs a person can do, and it requires an unselfish, committed, and loving person to do it successfully. Let your parents know how grateful you are for them as often as you can.

54

Send unexpected notes to family/friends.

One of life's really pleasant surprises is to get a note when you aren't expecting it. Sending unexpected notes of gratitude to family and friends will brighten their days in a way that nothing else can. Be sure to use the word grateful in the note, as that makes it that much more meaningful.

55

Show appreciation at the dinner table.

When I was growing up, a family dinner every night was the typical routine. Now that family dinner time has dropped in frequency, still remember to express your gratitude when you do sit down for dinner with your family. It is such a great time to communicate and express gratitude at the same time.

56

Give encouragement to someone in need.

When you focus on all that you have in your life, one of the things you notice is how fortunate you really are. Make the time to spread gratitude and give encouragement to people who aren't as fortunate as you. By helping someone else, you are letting your actions do the talking, and anyone would appreciate your kindness.

57

Compliment deserving people genuinely and frequently.

Sometimes people forget to show gratitude to the people who deserve it the most. People say," They already know how much I appreciate them," but you can never show too much gratitude toward anyone. Give genuine compliments often and with great sincerity. Do you ever get tired of hearing a compliment?

58

Call two family/friends each week.

Regardless of all of the forms of communication available today, there is still nothing like getting a phone call. Take the time to reach out to family or friends with a telephone call to see how they are and let them know how grateful you are to have them in your life.

59

It's not just a holiday thing.

Gratitude may be closely linked to the holiday of Thanksgiving because you are focusing on giving thanks. Remember to express your feelings of appreciation regardless of the season. Whether it is Christmas, or any other holiday, be sure to express your gratitude throughout the year.

60

Write a handwritten letter of thanks.

Surveys have proven that there is still nothing that connects to your brain any better than the written word. There was a time when everyone looked forward to receiving handwritten letters in the mail. Use a handwritten note to a friend to express your gratitude. They will remember it a lot longer and it will be so much more meaningful.

Gratitude Turns Your Blessings into Enough

61

Challenges become doable with gratitude's help.

Life is a series of ups and downs somewhat like the path of the roller coaster. When you are challenged with difficult situations, embracing gratitude will make the journey to the other side of the challenge that much easier. By focusing on your strengths, positives, and blessings, the challenge becomes a lot more doable.

62

Focus on all that you have.

Embracing a gratitude mindset helps you to focus on all that you have. It automatically programs your brain to see the glass as half-full. Using gratitude helps your brain to focus on the solution rather than the problem.

63

See every day as a blessing.

Someone once said that any day you wake up and you are alive is a good day. Life is very precious and any day above the ground is cause for celebration. Be very aware of the present and focus on it by celebrating your gratitude and blessings.

64

Recognize how good things really are.

For some reason, there are people on this earth who just see the negative side of things. I once said, “Good morning” to my father, and he responded, “What’s good about it?” Choose to be positive. With an “attitude of gratitude” you will more consistently see the good in everything you encounter.

65

Change to a mindset of abundance.

Planting seeds of gratitude in your mind will lead you to an abundant mindset. The abundance mindset is always looking for ways to accomplish things based on the current inventory of thoughts in your head. It points you in the direction of being a problem-solver.

66

You are free to make decisions.

No one controls your mind and your thoughts except you. When you are approaching your life from a position of strength, you are free to make your own decisions. Additionally, your decisions will be better because you are seeing the benefits of gratitude thinking.

67

Expressing gratitude will help create peace.

If you ask a lot of people what they are looking for, a number of them will say they are looking for peace. When you clear out your brain of the clutter caused by negative thoughts, you will find a much quicker road to a peaceful mind. Eliminating baggage makes the trip that much better.

68

Take time to connect with grace.

Being grateful will give you a better understanding of living your life with grace. The ability to put others' needs in front of yours. Having grace means God's favor. Connecting with grace will deepen your relationships and make you more open to new ones every day.

69

Lifelong tattoos can be great reminders.

Tattoos have become commonplace over the last few years. Many people today are sharing their feelings through tattoos. A lifelong tattoo can remind you each day of how grateful you are to have the blessings that you have in your life.

70

My true self is always grateful.

When you look in the mirror, it is such a great way to reflect on the image and think about the relationship you have with yourself. The person in the mirror is the one who can be the most grateful if you remind yourself each day. Try reconfirming the gratitude for your true self when you are brushing your teeth.

Creating Appreciation with Gratitude's Immense Power

71

Say thank you instead of yes.

There may not be two more important words to use when expressing your feelings of gratitude than "thank you." Those two small words can be so powerful when communicating the appreciation, you feel to another person after they have done something nice for you. You can say yes, but thank you is better.

72

Change your life? Change your life!

People often express their dissatisfaction with their lives and seem perplexed as to what to do. If you want to change your life, change your life. It does mean doing things differently, and one of the best ways to do things differently is to start looking at your life with a gratitude mindset. Shifting your mindset will help to actually change your life.

73

Smile more to break your pattern.

Your face is like a window to your mind. Remember to smile and to communicate to yourself and others that you have a positive mindset. Embracing gratitude will help keep that smile genuine and keep it on your face more often.

74

We all want the same thing.

Ultimately, I think everyone is looking for happiness and contentment in some form. It is very hard to get to those places when you come from a position of lack. By focusing on your abundance and gratitude, you too will get to a place happiness and contentment.

75

Your path to a grateful life

Like any path in life, it is not a straight line. It is filled with ups and downs and hills and valleys. Your gratitude mindset will help you to smooth out the valleys and overcome the down times. You will constantly focus on the goal regardless of the obstacles along the way.

76

It's called present for a reason.

Yesterday is gone and tomorrow isn't here yet. All you really have is this moment, the present. It's called the present because this moment is your moment, a present, a gift. Being grateful helps you to live in the present moment.

77

Embrace your mistakes; they're life's teacher.

Nobody likes to make mistakes, but they do us a big favor by teaching us about life. When you are grateful, your mistakes are viewed as instructive and not destructive. Your self-talk is so much more positive when gratitude shows you the benefits of your mistakes.

78

Unplug, spend more time in nature.

Another way to really plant gratitude into your brain is to get out in nature. Seeing what mother earth has provided for us will reinforce a gratitude mindset. The beauty and magnificence of nature will remind you why it is so important to be grateful.

79

Gratitude cures the huge entitlement problem.

Today's generation seems to feel very entitled. It's as if everything is owed to them. Once a person starts looking at all that they have, the sense of entitlement will go away. There's something about looking at all that you are grateful for that makes you appreciate your life, your blessings, and your abundance that much more.

80

Learn how to take a compliment.

When someone expresses their gratitude for you, be sure that you acknowledge that compliment properly. I was taught that there are two, and only two ways to accept a compliment. The first way is to simply say, "thank you." The second way is to say, "thank you, that's very nice of you to say." That's it--no exceptions. Learn how to take a compliment.

Weekly, Monthly, Yearly Symbols of Gratitude

81

Donate money to your favorite charity.

One of the ways that you can express gratitude is to give money to your favorite causes, charities, or philanthropic organizations. It becomes such a nice way to expand your reach and show gratitude in multiple ways.

82

Volunteer your time to a cause.

Another way to express gratitude is to volunteer your time. Time is the one thing that everyone has an equal amount of. When you volunteer your time, you express gratitude by giving away one of your most important assets--your time.

83

Practice daily activities for your health.

There is little that is more important than your health, because when you don't have your health, you don't have much. Be grateful for your health and plan daily activities that keep your mind and body healthy. Think about your exercise, diet, gratitude journal, meditation practice, and anything else that keeps your mind healthy and grateful.

84

Surround yourself with very supportive people.

It is said that "We are known by the company we keep." Be aware of who you are spending time with and ask yourself if they have a gratitude mindset. They say birds of a feather flock together and there is a reason for that. People with similar views toward gratitude will strengthen your view as well.

85

Be assertive, not aggressive, when needed.

When spreading the word about gratitude, show and tell people the real-life benefits of how and why it works. There is no need to be aggressive, as that will just send a person in the opposite direction. The example you set will be the best teacher.

86

Seek out and celebrate small victories.

It seems that nothing in this life is 100 percent. So, if there are to be good and bad happenings, seek out and celebrate the small victories along the way. Focusing on your abundance and gratitude will direct you to find even more wins in the game of life.

87

Be there when people need you.

They say that people only call you when they need something. By using gratitude's principles, you will not fall into that trap. Be the person who is there when they need you regardless of the situation.

88

Find a deserving person to mentor.

Many young people don't have the benefit of a father or mother. Find a young person to mentor and show them the power of gratitude. You will be forever changed by helping them to see what had not been provided for them before. It is one of the most powerful things you can do--help someone else.

89

Use exercise to stay extra positive.

Being grateful for your body means taking care of it. Daily exercise is very important to keep your body fit and feeling good, and it helps you to feel more positive. Just like your daily gratitude journal, make exercise part of your daily routine.

90

Teach by example, show the way.

Arguably the best technique for raising children or managing people is to set a great example. Let your gratitude practice set the example for the people in your life. Children and employees watch what you do. Always set a great example.

Share Gratitude and Spread the Word

91

Share your gratitude belief with others.

Anytime you share an experience, you enhance the feeling about that experience. By setting the example, the people around you will note the change in your attitude or belief and will have a tendency to follow you. Just like the life of the party, they will want a piece of what you have.

92

Spread the message, increase the feeling.

If you impact a percentage of the people you talk to about gratitude, then a larger group of people will represent a larger group of people impacted. Keep talking about gratitude and what it can do for your life. You will continue to expand your reach and influence.

93

Text someone to emphasize their value.

Take a moment to send a text every day to someone who would love to hear from you. Texts are a great way to communicate your gratitude and appreciation quickly and effectively. You can send them any time of day and for any reason. The impact can be huge, maybe even more than you know.

94

In helping others, you help yourself.

Nothing drives me more than the fact that if you want to help yourself, help others. With gratitude you remain strong and can assist those less able or less fortunate than you. One of the best feelings is knowing you made a difference in someone's life. By helping others, you will impact people far beyond what you realize.

95

Spread stories of gratitude's immense power.

The more a story is shared, the more it can be of value to many people. It's as if the story gains in meaning every time it is retold. When you hear about a story that illustrates the power of gratitude, pass it on to others.

96

Listen to friends' stories of hope.

I have already talked about the power of being a good listener. Encourage your friends to talk about their stories of hope and express to them how gratitude can assist them in overcoming challenges. Let them know that gratitude will help them along.

97

Become a great and interested listener.

As you become a great listener, listen to understand and not to respond. Ask great questions and let them talk and don't interrupt them. If you are a great and interested listener, people will think you are the nicest person they ever met.

98

Sharing gratitude enhances the experience exponentially

When you share with others, the experience is way beyond what you might expect. Just like when something really good or bad happens to you, the first thing you think about is who to share it with. Being grateful will always enhance the experience exponentially.

99

Share your vision for your future.

Let people know where you are going and how a gratitude mindset helped you get there. Whether it's the mindset, your daily gratitude journal, or anything that directed you with gratitude, know that you will inspire others with your vision, goals, or journey forward, enhanced by gratitude.

100

Lead others to their dreams/visions.

The best way to lead is to set an example of the behavior that you want modeled. By setting an excellent example, you will naturally lead others to their dreams and visions. There is no better feeling than helping someone else achieve their goals. You cannot put a price on impacting other lives as it is simply priceless.

About the Six-Word Lessons Series

Legend has it that Ernest Hemingway was challenged to write a story using only six words. He responded with the story, "For sale: baby shoes, never worn." The story tickles the imagination. Why were the shoes never worn? The answers are left up to the reader's imagination.

This style of writing has a number of aliases: postcard fiction, flash fiction, and micro fiction. Lonnie Pacelli was introduced to this concept in 2009 by a friend, and started thinking about how this extreme brevity could apply to today's communication culture of text messages, tweets and Facebook posts. He wrote the first book, *Six-Word Lessons for Project Managers*, then he and his wife Patty started helping other authors write and publish their own books in the series.

The books all have six-word chapters with six-word lesson titles, each followed by a one-page description. They can be written by entrepreneurs who want to promote their businesses, or anyone with a message to share.

See the entire ***Six-Word Lessons Series*** at **6wordlessons.com**

Made in the USA
Monee, IL
02 October 2022